Living on a PEG

by Jack Teeter

Prologue

I woke up At 3:45 this morning with a lot on my mind. I am a new Home Enteral Nutrition (HEN) patient. 'Enteral Nutrition': a way to deliver nutrients through a tube if you cannot take food or drink through your mouth. There's so much to learn, so many new things I need to know to take care of myself. It can be overwhelming.

Dr. O'Brien gave me a couple of instruction pamphlets to read. 'Percutaneous Endoscopic Gastrostomy', there's a tongue-twister for you. 60-ml syringes, disposable oral swabs, pill crushers; I'll be a walking chemistry experiment.

My wife and sons are being very positive through all this. And Sara, one of the night-shift nurses, told me about the *Oley Foundation* website where I can browse their forums for information and encouragement from other HEN patients. So, I've got a good support system. I'll get through this; try not to worry too much about the future,

stay focused on what I need to do to get through today –
when they implant my new PEG tube.

Here's my story: "I'm a 20-year throat cancer
survivor. Surgery, radiation, the whole nine yards. But,
along the way, the radiation has caused problems. First, I
developed radiation neuropathy. Pain in my neck and my
right shoulder was devastating... Whoa! This is getting
way too complicated.

Tell you what, this story will be easier if I make it
about fictitious people. Meet Sonny & Jenny Jacobs and
their son Jake:

Chapter 1

The little white two-story farm house sits on a long, narrow lot on North Street in downtown Brighton. If it's true that the top three measures of a home's value are location, location, and location, then the Jacobs' house rates right up there. Two blocks to the east is Broadway. On the four corners of North and Broadway are the town library, Brighton Pharmacy, First Bank, and a pizza place. One block west of their little house is Maple Street, otherwise known as highway 111. Within two blocks north or south on 111 are a Shell station, a Casey's convenience store/gas station, Tom's Grocery, a Dollar General store, Granny's restaurant, Targhetta Funeral Home, and a hardware store. Everything a person needs is within easy walking distance. 209 North Street, in this small town of 2300 people, is a convenient and peaceful place to live.

"Okay, Mother dear, who called this meeting?" Jake says, walking up the driveway. He joins his mother on the back porch on a beautiful Tuesday evening. She has a Sam Adams waiting for him on the little Plexiglas table between two deep-cushioned outdoor chairs.

"That would be me," she answers. She hands him the beer, but is obviously distracted. Her hair is down. She's wearing white shorts and a gray Tee with a *Rams* logo; very dressed-down for Jenny.

In jeans and a khaki Ford dealership-supplied uniform shirt with his name stitched over the left breast pocket, Jake clearly has worked late this evening. He screws off the top and takes a swig. "Cheers," he says, raising his bottle to tap his mother's Styrofoam cup of Pepsi. "You look like you're a million miles away. Are you all right?"

"Let's just sit a few minutes, Son. Your father is in the early innings of a Cardinal's game. He won't even know you're here."

"So, talk to me, Mom."

***

Earlier that morning, Jenny went with her husband to the doctor's office; more out of curiosity than concern. On a trip to their old stomping grounds in Oak Ridge Tennessee, Rachel, a sorority sister of Jenny's from back in the day, had given Sonny a half-empty bottle of pills. A new pain medicine called Lyrica. It helped Rachel manage her fibromyalgia, and Sonny felt immediate relief from the very first pill he took! Now, after peeling the label from the plastic pill container, Jenny was curious how Sonny would pull off bringing in an unlabeled prescription bottle to get a refill.

Dr. Elizabeth O'Brien, their new doctor since moving to Brighton, looked sideways at her patient. "I don't suppose I need ask where you got these?" she said. Dr. O'Brien is in her early 40's, appealing in a pudgy matronly sort of way. Both Jenny and Sonny have visited the doctor a number of times; she has a friendly, accepting demeanor and Jenny is convinced she knows her stuff.

"Better you shouldn't know," Sonny answered.

"Okay," O'Brien said, glancing over at Jenny. Jenny smiled warmly, rolled her eyes, and shrugged. "Well," the doctor continued, "Lyrica is to be taken three times daily with your meals. Is it working well for you?"

"It's better than what I was taking," Sonny told her. "That Neurontin I was on made me tired and *stupid*."

"And it works well with your neurostimulator?"

"So far, so good," said Sonny. "The Lyrica still makes me tired but in a more controlled way. Just a nap in the afternoon instead of nodding off every time I sit down. And it doesn't make me dopey. What a blessing to be able to think straight!"

Sonny has a neurostimulator implant, a medical device that overrides the pain messages to his brain. He takes pain pills to take the edge off the jolts from the neurostimulator.

"I still have problems when the weather changes, though. Saturday, on the drive home from Oak Ridge, we hit a storm outside of Lexington and I was beeping my neurostimulator like a fool. The clouds cleared off about half way across Kentucky and I beeped back down."

"I don't want you to think Lyrica will do away with mood swings or reaction to stress," Dr. O'Brien said. She ignored his reference to the trip back to Oak Ridge; the less she knew about how her patient obtained an unmarked prescription bottle containing twelve 75-mg tablets of Lyrica, the better. "Pain management is a process," she continued, staying on track, "it doesn't ever go away."

Dr. O'Brien smiled, making an entry on the clipboard she had carried into the examining room. "I'll have Sandy call in your new prescription."

***

"That sounds like it went okay, Mom." Jake looks full into her face again, trying to read what's hidden there.

Jenny sighs, making an effort to straighten her slumping shoulders. "You know how it is, son. No drug is ever *the* answer. Like Dr. O'Brien said: it's a process."

"Yeah, I guess so. But I'm sure glad Rachel gave Dad those pills to try. Even if it was illegal." Jake rises, reaching his hand out to his mother. "Day to day, Mom, right?"

"Day to day," she says, pulling up from her chair and patting her son's cheek. She picks up her cup and his beer bottle.

"Tell Dad I'll stop by again tomorrow," Jake says, going down the porch step to the driveway. As he opens his truck door, he adds: "Hey, get him to eat, will you? He looks like he's lost ten pounds just in the last month or so."

Jenny waves. "I'll fatten him back up, Jake. Don't you worry!"

***

She decides to stay out on the porch awhile, sitting back down heavily. *I'll fatten him back up. Don't you worry!*

Jenny sits for a very long time, remembering what else went on at the doctor's office this morning. The part she left out when she was relating the visit to her son.

***

Dr. O'Brien did smile, and she did say, "I'll have Sandy call in your new prescription." But that was not the end of Sonny's doctor visit.

"Now," she said, "let's get you up here on the examining table."

Sonny complied.

The doctor took her time: shining her little light in his ears, examining inside Sonny's mouth, running her fingers along the margins of his neck feeling his lymph nodes. She moved her stethoscope from round her neck to her ears, working in front first. Sonny took a deep breath. "Not yet," she said. "Just breathe normally." Working her way around to his shoulder blades: "Now slowly, in and out; deep breaths." She worked her way on down her patient's back. Sometimes listening more than once, asking him to take yet another breath.

"All right," she said, "now let's talk about the weight loss." She glanced over at Jenny to include her in the conversation. "Sonny, you were in the lab three weeks ago for a TSH test to see how the Synthroid was working."

"Sandy called and said the results were fine. He's taking the correct dosage," Jenny said.

"Yes," O'Brien said. "But we weighed you then, Sonny, like we do every time. You weighed two-oh-seven. Today you weighed in at one-ninety-four. That's a loss of thirteen pounds."

"Well, I've--"

"Not yet," the doctor said, "let me finish. Your lungs: down deep, there's some rattling." She paused, thinking of something else. She stepped to the examination room door calling, "Sandy, would you bring in an oximeter, please?"

"Hey, they put one of those on my finger when I was in the hospital for the neurostimulator implanr," Sonny said. "Measures the oxygen in your blood, right?" He let Sandy slip it on his index finger.

In a moment: "Eighty-nine," Sandy read. "Now take a few deep breaths."

He did.

Sandy turned to Dr. O'Brien. "Eighty-nine, doctor. Stayed right there."

Jenny and Sonny were both studying the doctor's face for answers. "Thanks, Sandy," she said. Sandy left, closing the door. "Ninety is borderline, Sonny. With the amount you exercise, normal for you should be ninety-six, easily."

The couple looked at her waiting for more information. "So, I've read the complete file you brought from Oak Ridge and from Nashville/Vanderbilt. You lost some weight from before your initial surgery but after all procedures you'd regained back to two-fifteen." She paused giving them time to digest the information.

"Now, we're hearing some pronounced crackling in your lower lungs. You've always had a bit of rattling, probably due to prolonged use of the tracheostomy tube in your stoma after the initial cancer surgery."

"Okay," Jenny said, looking at Sonny. "We're with you so far."

Dr. O'Brien waited, saying nothing.

"Sonny," Jenny said. "Can we talk about this?"

He nodded, lowering his head. "You go ahead."

Jenny got up from her chair and held her husband's hand. "He's been coughing."

"Go on," O'Brien said.

"When he eats."

Again the doctor waited.

"Sometimes a few bites go down, not too much coughing. But most other times--"

Sonny finally raised his head. "It feels like..." he said, "it feels like I have to cough and swallow, then cough and swallow again, sometimes several times before I can get it down. Sometimes I just give up and stop eating."

"Have you run across the term 'aspirating' in your medical history? Do you know what the term means?"

Jenny nudged her husband "Our friend Wilfred had that, remember, Sonny? He got pneumonia because he was aspirating."

Sonny looked up at Dr. O'Brien. "It means the food's going down the wrong pipe, right? Is that what's happening to me?" He wanted to look away but kept his gaze steady. "How bad is it? Does the uh, rattling mean I have pneumonia?"

She shook her head. "I'm not certain, yet. That eighty-nine percent blood oxygen level is especially worrisome. It means you're not getting enough oxygen. It may be because your aspirating has caused a buildup of fluid in your lungs." She picked up her clipboard, making another entry. "I'm going to set you up with a speech pathologist; tomorrow if possible. We can't let this get any further ahead of us."

"A speech pathologist?" Jenny asked.

The doctor set her clipboard back on the counter. She liked to use her hands when she spoke. "Let me explain the procedure…"

***

Pam, the office assistant for Dr. O'Brien, called Jenny at home about 4:00 that afternoon to tell them to report to the radiology department at Carlinville Hospital at 7:30 am tomorrow, Wednesday.

In about thirty minutes Sonny is up and around from his nap. Jenny is sitting on the living room couch reading a Dick Francis novel. "Pam called from Dr. O'Brien's office," she says.

He walks by her, making his way to the kitchen. "Just a minute, I need a Coke. My mouth tastes like a sewer. You want anything?"

"No thanks."

Settling back into his straight-backed chair: "Okay, Darlin', whatcha got?" Really thirsty, he takes a big swig of his Coke.

WHOOSH!

The thick liquid comes rushing back out his nose as well as his mouth. His T-shirt is soaked. He nearly spills the rest of the contents of the can before setting it on the coaster on the end table next to him. "Well, damn! Ain't this a mess!"

Chapter 2

"I'm Sonny Jacobs." Sonny reports with his wife, right on time, to the radiology department. He and Jenny have already stopped by registration to get Dr. O'Brien's paperwork.

The pleasant woman behind the glass enclosure, looking much more alert and awake than Sonny feels this morning, accepts his paperwork. She tears off a small pink sheet and hands it back to him, pointing back around the corner. "Go across the hall there, please. We have to do a lab procedure first."

"I'll stay out here," Jenny says, taking a seat in the waiting area.

A slightly-built Hispanic woman, her hands at work with some glassware in the sink, hears Sonny come in. She has her back to him. "I'll be right with you."

He's been here before. He takes a seat in what looks like an over-sized school desk with wide, fold-down wings.

He pulls up the left wing of the chair and sets his arm on it. His best vein is on his left side, in the crook of his elbow.

Carla, her name tag reads, turns to greet him and takes his paper, glancing for his name. "Ah, so we meet again, Mr. Jacobs. Got that big old vein all ready for me, I see."

"Yep," Sonny says, "howya doin' today, Carla?"

"Fine, Mr. Jacobs. Now make a fist for me."

"What's this test for?"

"Liver, make sure you can handle the barium they use to make the stuff you swallow show up on the x-ray. Did Dr. O'Brien tell you how the test works?"

"She did."

In moments the lab clinician has all the blood she needs. "Okay, you know the drill. Elevate your arm and give me some pressure on this gauze."

"How long's the wait?"

"I'll have the results ready for radiology in 15 minutes or so."

"Great." Sonny stands up after she places a wrap over the gauze. "Thanks, Carla, see ya."

"Take care, Mr. Jacobs."

"Liver test for the barium," Sonny says, sitting down next to his wife.

Jenny has her nose in a *Mademoiselle* magazine. "Uh huh." There's no one else in the waiting area this early. Jenny wonders if they fit Sonny in, at Dr. O'Brien request, before today's regular schedule.

Sonny makes an adjustment on the controller of his neurostimulator, causing the controller to make a single beeping sound, then settles in. He's brought a James Burke novel.

"Jacobs," a tall thin blond woman in purple scrubs hails, opening the double doors.

Sonny and Jenny both rise. "Am I allowed to watch the procedure?" Jenny asks.

"Sure, come ahead." Her name tag reads: Doris. "Follow me, please."

Sonny takes a seat next to an x–ray machine set at throat level. "The procedure will be recorded," the nurse says, gesturing at a monitor mounted on the wall at the far end of the room, near where Jenny takes a seat.

On a counter, close to where Sonny is seated, a serving tray contains several small plastic cups of various edibles. An inverted stack of paper Dixie cups is alongside.

Jenny's plastic chair is located so she can view the monitor and hear what's going on, but out of range of the x-rays.

After the barium is injected, a technician takes his place on the other side of the x-ray machine. The tech is an older man with a buzz cut and a trimmed goatee. His face is chiseled. He's lean, but not skinny. He's wearing a lead vest and pleasant expression.

The speech therapist takes her place in front of Sonny, introducing herself but not offering her hand because she's wearing latex gloves. "I'm Dr. Keoni" She nods in Jenny's direction. "Nice to see you both on this early morning."

"Howya, doin'?" Sonny says, holding up the controller for his neurostimulator. "I have a neurostimulator, a wire in my spine for pain control. Is it going to bother this procedure? Do I need to turn it off?"

"Should be okay," the tech says. "This is an x-ray, not an MRI."

"Well, there's your answer. Thanks, Bill." Dr. Keoni nods in his direction. "Bill Hostedler, meet the Jacobs."

Bill nods, waves at Jenny over in the corner. Sonny puts the controller back in his jeans pocket.

Dr. Keoni is Asian; petite in stature but taut in her mannerisms; all business. She is graceful in her movements, her hands testing the tautness of the flesh of Sonny's neck, the size and position of his Adam's apple. And like Dr. O'Brien did yesterday, she tests Sonny's lymph areas. When she is done: "Dr. O'Brien explained what we're about this morning?"

"Yes." Sonny says.

"All right let's get started." She stands directly in front of him, studying the movements of his neck and mouth. "Could you please say -- slowly now: 'He fixed the roof after it leaked.'"

"He fixed the roof after it leaked."

"Fine. And now: 'The boy gave the girl an ice cream.'"

Sonny complies.

"Good," Dr. Keoni says, moving to the tray. She dips a wooden ice cream spoon into a cup containing something yellow-gold; looks like honey. She returns to stand directly in front of him. "All right, now let me see you swallow a few times. Close your mouth and work your throat for me -- swallow."

Sonny does so, several times.

The screen on the wall shows this activity. Jenny studies it from her position but can't decipher what she's seeing.

"Fine," the therapist says. "Now, I'm going to hand you this spoonful of honey. Spoon it into your mouth and swallow."

The honey feels cool and smooth in his mouth. As it leaves his mouth he moves his throat muscles to swallow.

Nothing happens. It's as if the honey has evaporated in his throat. Dr. Keoni studies his throat movements.

Jenny watches the monitor. As she watches, the honey glides down, seemingly unrestricted, not controlled.

Sonny makes the effort to swallow several more times. Still, nothing happens. Dr. Keoni continues to observe his throat movements.

"Now cough please, Mr. Jacobs."

Sonny does. He feels most of the honey come back up into his mouth.

The doctor reaches for a Dixie cup and hands it to Sonny, taking back the wooden spoon and discarding it. "And spit into this cup please, Mr. Jacobs."

Sonny spits out the honey. His stunned expression betrays his sense of helplessness.

I'm confused. Jenny can't begin to understand what she has seen on the monitor. *No, not confused,* she decides, *I'm terrified!*

"All right, Mr. Jacobs," the therapist says, taking the cup from him. Her demeanor is firm, her tone steady. "Now stand up please and we'll join your wife in front of the monitor."

Jenny stands to join them.

When they are in place: "Bill, run it back for us, please." She approaches the monitor, pointing at the mass of honey. "Now, Mr. Jacobs, when I was watching the muscles in your throat you were making every effort to swallow. The muscles were functioning correctly. There was every external indication that you were guiding that honey down into your esophagus."

Jenny grasps Sonny's hand, interlocking their fingers, squeezing tightly. *Swallow* - she urges the image before her -- *swallow*! But the honey doesn't break up, doesn't separate. It stays in the same glob shape as it enters -- gliding -- driven only by gravity, down, down and down.

"But as you can see," Dr. Keoni continues. "Only gravity is controlling the flow. Your epiglottis has no perception that a bolus of food is making its way down."

Abruptly, Sonny pulls his hand away from his wife. "Give me a couple of minutes," he says. He walks determinedly down the hall and away.

Jenny watches him go. "He needs some time to himself," she says to the doctor, sitting back down, "he'll be back in a few minutes." She returns to the plastic chair.

The doctor and technician busy themselves with something at the other end of the room near the x-ray machine, giving Jenny a moment alone.

He'll get through this, Jenny tells herself. Some*how, some way, we'll both get through this*!

After several long moments, Sonny comes back in. His expression is impassive, his posture stoic. He walks over to Jenny, pulls her up to him, holding his wife in his arms. They stand that way for a long time, simply holding each other.

Finally, Sonny straightens. "Doctor?"

"Yes?" she approaches.

"Are there any more tests?"

"I'd like to do the same test with something a little more solid and then just a trial run with a sip of water. Are you up to that now?"

"Yes," Sonny answers, touching his wife's cheek and returning to the seat beside the x-ray machine.

"Are you all right, Mrs. Jacobs?" Dr. Keoni asks. "Can we get you anything, some water perhaps?"

"Nothing, thank you, I'm okay." Jenny says.

She turns to walk from the room, toward the entrance hallway. At the doorway she pauses. "I'll be right outside, Honey," she says. "I won't be far."

As she leaves, Sonny massages his face with his palms. Having forgotten all about his neurostimulator, he decides a single beep might help get him through the next few minutes. He makes the adjustment then puts the controller back in his pocket.

"Let's do this, Dr. Keoni."

***

About an hour after the couple returns home, Jenny receives a phone call. "This is Pam calling from Dr. O'Brien's office. Can you hold for the doctor please?"

Jenny waits. Sonny is gone for a walk. There is a clicking sound and the doctor is on the line. "Mrs. Jacobs..." Dr. O'Brien hesitates a moment, softening her tone. "*Jenny*... I've received the report from Dr. Keoni."

"Well, that was fast."

"Yes, we're not wasting any time if we can help it. We need to get your husband..." Again she hesitates, her voice straining for a compassionate tone. "We need to get *Sonny* admitted to the hospital right away."

Jenny sighs, recognizing the inevitability of this call. "Sonny's out for a walk right now. We have an appointment with a lawyer after lunch. Should we go ahead and keep that appointment or --"

She stops herself. "Wait, he won't be able to eat any lunch will he?"

"I'd assume not," Dr. O'Brien says. "We really didn't know until Dr. Keoni's report, but at this point Sonny's apparently not getting *anything* into his digestive system; and that includes even water. He shouldn't be out walking around right now. He's almost certainly dehydrated or very nearly so."

"So, I should go get him? Bring him now?" Jenny's voice is an octave higher than usual. She finds it hard to catch her breath.

"Absolutely. Call an ambulance if you think there's any sign of weakness or shortness of breath. Otherwise, you should see to it that he's at Carlinville hospital no later than…" There's a pause, Jenny assumes she's looking at her watch. "It's nearly twelve-thirty now. And you have a half-hour drive. We'll call to make sure he can be admitted by as early as one o'clock. Take him to the emergency room and they'll get him on an IV to ward off the dehydration and admit him."

"You're going to meet us there?"

"I'll be making rounds late this afternoon. He'll be well taken care of by the admitting staff."

Suddenly Jenny realizes there's no more time for questions. Her imagination is running like crazy! *He could be lying in a ditch right now!* "Listen, I've got to go. Goodbye."

***

Only two blocks east from the Jacobs' house, catty-corner from the library, there's a low, cold concrete bench. The bench is a good place to watch the freight and passenger trains that pass through the middle of town. There is no station in Brighton, trains blow their whistles at the crossing and move on through without even slowing down. Jenny finds Sonny sitting on that concrete bench, facing out across the tracks.

Jenny pulls into the library parking lot. Every nerve in her body is jangling. She wants to jump from the car while it's still moving, leaving the motor running, door ajar, and warning beeper beeping. But she doesn't. Safely parked, she calls to her husband as she crosses the empty street, "Hey handsome, waitin' for a train?"

Sonny turns at the sound of her voice. His expression is neutral, thoughtful. "Hey Babe, come sit beside me."

She does.

"Time to go, huh?" he says.

"Yes," she answers, calmly.

Sonny turns his gaze back out to the tracks. "Thinking about it, I kinda wondered why Dr. Keoni let us leave the hospital."

Jenny slips her arm inside his. "Dr. O'Brien got a fast turnaround on the results. She called to say you should be admitted right away. How are you feeling?"

Sonny shrugs. "No different than usual, really. But us coaches know all about dehydration. I've seen it come upon kids all of a sudden. One minute they're running sprints, then the next minute they're lying on the grass before they know what hit 'em."

She gives his arm a gentle tug. "So, you ready?"

He moves his right hand across and takes hers, under his arm. "I don't guess a couple minutes will matter either way. Let me tell you what I was thinking about."

"Sure," Jenny says, settling back against him.

He gestures with a movement of his neck at the tracks before him. "I don't think I ever told you this story, Jenny.

"When I was a little tyke, probably first grade, the teacher told us to draw a railroad track, from the bottom of the page up to the top. I did, all of us did. My picture was the same from bottom to top. The rails were the same thickness and the ties were the same length. The teacher walked around the room looking over shoulders. When she came to me she said, 'You drew a ladder, Sonny.'"

Jenny smiles her patient 'Ms. Jacobs, retired fifth grade school teacher' smile, encouraging him to go on.

He pulls away from her, only a small amount of space on the bench but enough to give his story room in his head. "I guess I wasn't the only kid who drew a ladder. Ms. McGovern – strange I just now remembered her name -- anyway, she went to the board and drew the picture the way all grown-ups know a railroad track should look: wide at the bottom and narrowing down to nothing at the top. For some reason her drawing made me sad that day. I didn't know why, but I was sad thinking about her picture for a long time.

"And sitting here, now, I thought about my *ladder* again," he says, finishing with a sigh. "And I'm sadder now than when I was in first grade."

Jenny didn't make any comment. She sat patiently, waiting for her husband to decide it was time to go.

***

"So, Coach," Jenny says as they glide along highway 111 on the way to Carlinville, "are you going to tell your team the deep existential meaning of your rambling little yarn, or are we supposed to figure it out on our own?"

Sonny chuckles. "Good melodrama is wasted on you, Babe. I'd have cut you on the first day of practice."

"You'd have missed my slider, Coach. Hitters swear it's so fast it looks like it's getting smaller the minute it leaves my hand."

"So…" Sonny says.

Jenny chuckles. "Young Mr. Jacobs likes to keep things wide open. Doesn't like things closing in on him."

"See there, you *do* get it. And they said you were all looks and no brains."

"So, you feel like you're running out of options?"

"Yeah, kinda."

"You know what my mother would have said about all this, don't you?"

"I do. She'd have said: 'When God closes a door, He opens a window.'" Sonny grins. "Then she'd start in with her crazy religious logic: 'You should be glad God gave you Lyrica to make your pain better. Now you'll be able to handle not eating.'

"Some trade, huh? No Meat-lover's pizza, Dunkin' Donuts, Litton's Red Velvet cake, McDonald's double cheeseburgers, House of Pancakes omelets, Sam Adams beer, Coke--"

Jenny taps at her left wrist as if there were a watch there. "Do you intend to list every food and drink available in America?"

"Maybe later; I guess I've made my point. This is another 'quality of life' issue -- big time!"

"Want to hear what Jake said when he was worrying about you losing weight?"

"What?"

"He said, 'Day to day, Mom; day to day.'"

"Wait, I know that song." Sonny plays an air guitar. "One day at a time, sweet Jesus, that's all I'm askin' of you!"

"Well, it's true. What other options do we have, Sonny?"

"That's what I was thinking about on the bench near the railroad tracks. Those commuter trains come through at over 60 miles an hour. I'd be like a bug on the windshield."

"Don't even go there, Sonny. Not even kidding around. What an awful thought."

Distracted by their discussion, they've made their way all the way to the Wal-Mart on the road in to Carlinville. "Just a few more blocks to go," Jenny says. "What's it gonna be: railroad tracks or the hospital?"

"I guess I'll give the old feeding tube another try. You remember I had one for about two months when I had that trachea tube and couldn't swallow after my cancer surgery."

"Oh, hey, now I *do* remember that! I was going *crazy* trying to figure out how they were going to get food into you. I forgot all about that. That was a long time ago, Sonny. But we made it through that okay. See, things are looking brighter already!"

"I wonder if feeding tubes have changed any?"

"We're about to find out."

Chapter 3

Dr. O'Brien brings a 'peg' tube to Sonny's room for show and tell. "How are you doing this evening, Sonny?" she asks.

"I'm good," he answers, smiling over at is wife in the guest chair on the window side of the room. "Jenny's ambulance service got me here before I got too dehydrated."

Her patient looks vigorous, with good color, and in good spirits. Sonny has an IV running steadily with a dextrose solution, to help balance his electrolytes and keep him hydrated; there's a nub near the IV site for injecting medication.

"So," Sonny says, "that's a 'peg' tube. How does it work?"

The doctor switches into 'information' mode. There's a lot to explain and the more clinical her language the better. "The shorter end is inserted through your stomach wall; the bulb down on the end is inflated inside your stomach to provide resistance to being pulled out. The disk will be on the outside to keep the tube snug and provide a base for the length of tube on the exterior."

"Why is it so long on the outside?"

"You'll find having this much length on the outside gives you room to manipulate in order to see what you're doing as you to learn to feed yourself."

Jenny has a question: "Won't it dangle down, like hang in the way when he's not feeding himself? If it gets under his belt the whole thing might get jerked out if he bends the wrong way."

"There *will* be an adjustment period to get the feel of having something hanging from your abdomen." Dr. O'Brien answers, keeping her focus on Sonny even though she's glad to answer his wife's questions, too. "It will take some getting used to, for instance, in the shower and when you're drying off. Generally though, for everyday walking around, you can tape it to the side on your abdomen to hold it in place. Or they make little pouches that hang from an elastic belt around your lower chest."

"Okay," Sonny says, toggling the device that changes the angle of the bed, allowing him sit up. "Why are there three of those capped plugs sticking out? Don't I only need one to feed myself?"

"Actually, only two of the plugs have caps that open for feeding. The idea would be if a patient were bedridden and force-fed through one plug, the other could be used to infuse medication, for instance. But in your case only one plug, the one in the middle, is sufficient. Now, the third plug has a special 'head' and is used to inflate the bulb inside your stomach."

"So don't mess with that one, right?"

"Right. Any other questions?" She looks over to include Jenny.

Sonny laughs. "Once that thing is inside me I'll have a million more. Oh, I know one: how soon after it goes in can I start using it?"

"After twenty-four hours you'll start with water. Next day you'll begin a regimen of feedings five times per day."

"Oh," Sonny says, thinking of another question. "Will it bleed around the hole in my stomach?"

"After the initial twenty-four hour period you won't have much discharge unless you put the unit under stress accidentally. Like any such surgical opening though, it's very important to keep the entire area clean and dry. One last thing:"

"Yes?"

"You will have help. The nurses will let you progress as quickly as you are able to take care of yourself. But they will monitor every feeding and cleaning around the site for a while to make sure everything goes well. And when you go home -- you'll be going home in four or five days -- a visiting nurse will be assigned to assure that everything is going well. Daily at first, then less often; and finally you'll be on your own completely."

"That's good to know," Sonny says. "So, I'll eat five times a day. That's like breakfast, lunch, and dinner, then what other times?"

"Most people get on a three-hour schedule. If you start at, say, seven AM that will make your last feeding at seven PM." She looks at Jenny again. "Your family can work their regular three-meals-a-day schedule around that so that you can be part of regular mealtime."

"What will he eat?" Jenny asks. "That tube looks kinda skinny. Is it like that *Ensure* stuff they show? You know diet supplements on TV?"

"It is *like* that. I'll prescribe a product called Jevity. It's a complete nutritional liquid supplement, always used under a physician's care." She turns back to Sonny. "Adjustments to what nutritional strength and what amount of Jevity you ingest each feeding will be made based on your body's tolerance and your caloric requirements to maintain body weight. Generally, you can expect to take one and one-half cans per feeding along with one-hundred twenty milliliters of water before and after the Jevity.

"You'll pressure-infuse the water using a sixty milliliter syringe because water is lighter than the Jevity and won't work by gravity flow. Also the water pressure helps clear the tube. You'll use an open syringe -- no plunger -- to infuse the Jevity. Pop the top on the can, pour it in, and let gravity do the work."

Sonny raises his index finger. "Hey, I know what else we forgot: my medications, my pills."

"Some medication comes in liquid form, but usually that's much more expensive. And medications like Lyrica don't come in a liquid form."

"So it'll be a chemistry experiment, kinda?"

"Yes. You'll open capsules or grind pills then mix them with water in a small cup. Then you'll draw the mixture up into your syringe and force-infuse it. Be sure to follow up any meds with a measure of forced clear water to clean the tube and to make sure that all the meds actually make their way through the tube."

Sonny closes his eyes for a moment, concentrating. "This is a lot to remember."

The doctor continues to be patient with her answers. "Your nurses, and later your home health care personnel, will help you get everything right. Once you establish a rhythm, a procedure, you'll be in complete control.

"Any more questions for now?"

"I have one," Jenny says. "Is this -- not being able to feel anything in his throat -- related to all the radiation after his first surgery? You know, like the pain in his neck and shoulders. Both of them seemed to come on a long time after."

Sonny nods. "That's what I'm thinking too, Babe. Problem is: there's no way to know for sure." He looks at Dr. O'Brien. "Isn't that right, Doctor?"

"That's right. Radiation therapy was a bit less um, directed -- less precise -- than today. This new condition could very well be related to that treatment." She gives herself a few minutes to think whether there's anything else to add to this analysis. There's not. "Well, any other questions about the upcoming procedure?"

"I'm good." Sonny gives Jenny the thumbs up sign. "When do they 'peg' me?"

"Bright and early tomorrow. One thing I want to warn you about. For that first twenty-four hours, you will not be infusing any medications. In your case that poses some discomfort without your Lyrica."

Sonny grimaces, looks out the window. "At least the weather is clear. My shoulder pain might not be too bad. I'll just have to tough it out, huh? Let my neurostimulator do the job?"

"That's the idea. Try to keep your mind busy during that initial period. There will be some site discomfort, too. It's best to have a good book handy, some favorite music to listen to, watch some good TV, whatever it takes. You won't get much rest."

"Okay. Tomorrow morning then, bright and early."

***

"Wake up Mr. Jacobs. Mr. Jacobs, wake up please. Oh, good there you are. It's time for your breathing treatment."

"Um… my what?" Sonny is groggy, feels like he's been asleep for hours. He turns his head to place the voice with a person.

The owner of the voice is a slight, graying man who looks like a professor. His eyes are friendly. He reaches back around Sonny's bed and plugs in something that makes a bubbling sound. When he comes back within view he has an oxygen mask in his hand. "Have you had a breathing treatment before?"

"Nope."

The bed begins to move to an upright seated position. "We've got to get you sitting up for this."

Sonny squirms around to accommodate the movement. "Breathing treatment?"

As the bed continues to adjust: "Yes Sir. We're going to put this mask over our mouth and nose and adjust this elastic band to make it fit. Then you're going to breathe as deeply as possible -- deep in, deep out -- for about twenty minutes."

The bed stops moving. 'Mark', his name tag reads, lets the bed controller go; it is wound around the bed railing to keep from dropping to the floor. "Okay," Sonny says. "What's in there? What's with the bubbling sound?"

The nurse adjusts the mask. "Nebulizer, the bubbling is filtering the treatment through water to keep your throat from drying out. The medication is to break up the fluid built up in your lungs. When you feel like coughing, just move the mask aside." Mark continues, as Sonny begins taking deep breaths as instructed. "The idea is to help you to cough up all that stuff in your lungs."

Sonny nods and continues the exercise.

"Deep, but not fast, Mr. Jacobs; you can slow the pace and relax." He turns to leave. "I'll be back in a few."

Always surprises in a hospital, Sonny thinks. *Breathe deep.*

Jenny comes back in about half way through the treatment. She's momentarily alarmed at the sight of the oxygen mask.

Sonny pulls it aside and mutters, "Breathing treatment."

"Oh," Jenny says, relaxing, not knowing exactly what a breathing treatment does but her husband seems fine with it. She sits down in the surprisingly comfortable hospital-green vinyl-covered chair and looks around. The building is brand new, less than a year old. For a 25-bed county hospital it is amazingly well equipped and well-staffed. Pictures in the main hallway show no fewer than 20 physician associates, including Dr. O'Brien. Every room is a single room. The number of plugs and dials and thing-a-ma-jigs behind each bed is impressive. Sonny is breathing away in his oxygen mask. Jenny takes up her book: a Dick

Francis novel. Quick read, easy to get back to if you're interrupted.

***

"This place is great!" Jake says, entering. He breaks into song: "Everything's up to date in Kansas City. They've gone about as fer as they can go."

He's wearing another version of his work uniform. This one has a wide black stripe with red-over-white trim across his chest and the arms of his shirt. Jenny had called after Sonny was admitted to fill him in on his father's aspiration, telling him that Sonny was being admitted to check for pneumonia symptoms. Jake walks over to embrace his mother, who stands to greet him. "Jeez Mom. You look like a million bucks, even in a hospital room."

And she does. Jenny's hair is styled in huge ringlets in the back with smaller ones surrounding her bright face. Her green eyes shine. She's wearing the same jeans and white blouse she started the day with but has found time to get her hair done. "I went to the beauty shop on the square while your father was napping earlier." She displays her hands. "They even had Corvette Red polish."

Sonny slides his legs out from under the covers and sits up on the side of the bed. "Howya doin', Son."

Jake moves to give his father a hug. "You look all right to me. How soon can we get you checked out of here?"

"Maybe wait a couple days. Gotta get my 'peg' tube first."

"'Peg' tube?" Jake looks sideways at his mother. "Mom, I thought you said--"

Sonny interrupts, "Hold on Son, don't blame your mother." He slides back around, searching for the button-on-a-chord that levers his bed up to the sitting position. He nods at his wife. "I asked your mother to let me tell you about. It's a tube they put in my belly to get nutrition into me. They're going to put it in tomorrow morning."

Jake needs more information. "And you need nutrition this way *because*?"

"Because I can't eat or drink, dammit!" Sonny yells. "And I ain't very happy about it either!"

Jake draws away. "Take my head off, why don't you, Dad."

Jenny hurries to take her son by the elbow. "Let's go get a soda in the cafeteria. Your father needs to calm down."

"I'm sorry, Jake," Sonny says, reaching to touch his son's shoulder as they turn to leave. He's calmer now. "This is all gonna take some getting used to."

Jake stops, turns around and returns to hug his father again, who by now has worked the bed into the sitting position. "I love you, Coach." He straightens to look his father in the eye. Jake's eyes are wet. Confused and uncomfortable, he glances at his watch. "Listen, maybe I better take a rain check on that Coke, Mom. Debbie will have already fed the kids, but she waits supper on me 'til the cows come home. I hate to keep her waiting."

Sonny swings his legs out from the bed again, standing to embrace his son. "Sorry I kept this from you. I wanted to tell you myself, in person."

"No sweat." Jake returns the hug warmly. "I'd react the same way if…" He doesn't finish his sentence. He turns to go. "Take care, Dad. Good luck with everything tomorrow."

Chapter 4

Sonny wakes up singing, at least trying to: "Please... let... way."

Jenny, glad to see him awake after two hours of waiting by his bedside, gets up from her chair to listen.

He makes a writing movement with his right hand and tries again, with even less success than the first time. His words are completely garbled. "pls... wa."

Jenny doesn't understand the first time he does his hand signal. But when he makes the sign again he holds his left hand flat under his writing hand -- obvious: he wants to write something. There's a 4-by-6 pad with the hospital logo on the window ledge. She digs around in her purse for a pen. She hands her husband the pen and pad, smiling. "Here you go, Honey. Mouth too dry to talk?"

Squirming around to get a base for writing from flat on his back, careful not to pull at the IV insert at his wrist, Sonny writes: 'YOU!' then hands the pad back. He makes another attempt at singing: "Please don't... go... way." This time, it *sounds* like singing -- to Sonny.

Jenny smiles and bends to nuzzle his neck. "I've got no idea what you're saying but I'm glad you're awake and communicating." She spies a spray container of Biotene in the oversize pink plastic bin that sits on his bedside tray. Reaching, she decides she's going to have to go around the bed.

She does; then takes the top off the spray bottle, handing it to him.

He takes it with his left hand and sprays his tongue a couple of times. "mmmnn... uhaaa... mmmnn--

"There that's better. Write this down, Babe before it gets away." He waits for her to scurry around to where she set her pad down. "Ready?"

Jenny nods, pen at the ready.

Please don't let the music go away

Sometimes, it's all I have

To make it through another day

He's singing! As she writes, Jenny's eyes mist up. *Oh my God! He's singing!* She blinks several times before raising her eyes to him after she finishes writing. She attempts nonchalance: "A new song, huh?"

Sonny waves her question away, anxious to get the whole chorus on paper. It's been a long time since he felt this urge to write. The fingers of his left hand itch for guitar strings; he has to get this down!

Lord, I know I don't deserve

A single song You gave

But please, don't let the music

Go away

"How do you like it, Jenny? I started thinking about it before I went to sleep last night. Then, it was the only... it was all I could dream about."

She reaches down to nuzzle him again. "So you're not groggy or anything? Are you in any pain?"

"Nah, I'm feeling pretty good." Sonny pulls back the blanket with his left hand. "Voila! My new 'peg' tube." The tube extends out from a hole in a 4-by-4 bandage. There's no swelling or redness around the bandage. Apparently, the procedure was localized and not too traumatic.

Struggling to be offhand, not go overboard – despite the shock of seeing a length of plastic tube hanging from her husband's abdomen – Jenny holds up the pad with the new lyrics. "So, what's this one about?"

Pulling his cover back in place, Sonny gazes out the window and winces involuntarily, looks around, finally spots his controller on the tray. Beeping once, he says, "Twenty-four hours until Lyrica. I managed to get my last one down about four-thirty this morning -- liked to gagged myself silly." He gestures with his chin at the window. "Rain, it'll probably rain for the next 48 hours. This low pressure isn't helping a bit. Why couldn't we have a nice dry high pressure system roll in?"

"I thought about you on the drive in. The forecast says rain until mid-morning tomorrow, Friday." She's still holding the pad up, waiting for an answer about the new song.

Suddenly Sonny is tired. He yawns and then starts coughing. It takes several Kleenex for spitting and lots more coughing to get back under control. "One positive thing, Babe, well two actually."

"Tell me. I don't see anything negative. The nurses say your 'peg' tube is looking fine and it's gonna save your life. To me, that's *very* positive."

Sonny reaches up to touch her lips with his fingertips. "You're right. I can get through twenty-four hours; especially with your help. Our old Oak Ridge pals Doug and Rachael calling last night was nice, too."

Jenny strokes the stubble on his cheek with the back of her hand. "Tell me about the new song."

"Oh, yeah. So, I was thinking about aspirating and all that. Then, that got me to thinking about... Well..."

"What?"

"Since I had my neurostimulator put in, I haven't done any writing. Feeling sorry for myself, I guess. Anyway, it's been a long time." He points to the pad. "I think this one's gonna be pretty good. That's just the chorus. I've got two lines of the first verse; just about there. Write this down, Babe:"

We wrote songs on yellow pads

And napkins in restaurants

She does.

He grins, gesturing again at the pad. "Now, stuff that in your purse and don't show it to anybody. Nobody sees or hears nothin' until we get this sucker copyrighted."

Jenny makes a grand gesture of folding the pad and putting the whole thing in her purse. She smiles proudly. "I like it, Honey. Especially that part about 'we don't deserve a single song You gave.'"

"I don't know, maybe... maybe music is a gift from God, whether singing or writing." He shrugs, and yawns again. Reaching his left hand over to grasp his wife's, he drifts off to sleep.

Even though Sonny is groggy the next few hours, his hospital life goes on. Jenny's stays with him, fighting sleep herself. She needs to stay alert; needs to pay strict attention to the changing of her husband's dressing. Sonny's very independent but she may have to help once they get home. Despite her best efforts, she drifts off to sleep in her chair...

After about half an hour of quiet, the overhead light is abruptly turned on to wake Sonny up. It's time for another breathing treatment. As soon as that's over, it's time for a nurse to look at the dressing around the 'peg' tube. "It's still all right," Jacqueline, the tiny dark-haired nurse says. "We'll leave it alone for a while." She takes Sonny's vitals. "All good. Is there anything I can get you, Mr. Jacobs? Is your bed comfortable or would you like to sit up a little higher?"

"I'm good," he says, "thanks, Jackie."

"I'll be back to check on you." She pauses near the light switch. "On or off?"

"Leave it on, please." Then to his wife: "Jenny, would you say we're religious?"

His wife is standing by his bedside. "I don't know, I guess. Why?" She turns to the window. "It's dark in here. Do you want me to open the blinds?"

"No thanks, I don't need any reminders that it's raining. So, I'm lying here, dozing off and on, can't really concentrate on my Burke book -- it's pretty good, by the way, Clete Purcell has gotten his butt kicked twice already -- so I was thinking about my songs. All of them, even this latest one, are at least uh, *somewhat* religious. I wonder why that is, since we don't even go to church."

"The answer to why we don't go to church is easy, Sonny."

"Yeah?"

"Yes, church is a *social* institution." She pauses for a moment. Her phone is vibrating. She pulls it from the pocket of her slacks and looks at the readout without answering. "Rachel," she tells Sonny. "I'll call her back.

"Where were we? Oh, I know: social. Churches have good and bad people; just like in any other social group. I think we've met *way* more than our fair share of bad church people. That's the answer for me anyway. What about you?"

"I agree. What about praying? I mean actually *talking* to God." He coughs a of couple times, sounding raspy. "I've done that a few times. But you know what? I can't remember ever trying to make any *deals* with God or asking 'why me'. Not even when I first got sick. But I have prayed."

"Everybody prays, like saying 'oh Jesus' unconsciously when something unexpected happens. Is that the kind of praying you mean?"

He chuckles. "That's not exactly what I meant."

"Well, I know one thing, Honey, I am *not* an 'alter call' Christian. You know, when they have that little session at the end of the service where the preacher asks you to search your heart. 'Search your heart.' Give me a break! That is *so* lame to me."

Sonny sighs and stirs around in bed, searching for a comfortable place for his butt. "Just seems weird, me being a Christian Country song writer but us not being religious." He laughs at a new thought: "So, there I am, up at the podium, accepting some music award: 'First of all, I want to thank God.' That wouldn't be very honest."

Jenny laughs with him. "This sounds like it might be a pretty good song, but it might be a little early to be thinking about awards. But I get your point." She pauses, looking into his tired eyes. "You sure you want to talk about all this?"

Sonny inhales deeply, coughing suddenly, several times, reaching for a Kleenex. When he's done: "I'll let you worry about it for now. I'm worn out again."

She holds her husband's hand as he drifts off to sleep.

Living On A PEG

Chapter 5

"Jenny this is such a nice surprise. You drove all the way home and back to--"

She reaches in her purse and retrieves a packet of guitar strings and his pitch pipe. "I found this stuff, too. I figured you'd like to have your guitar around to work on this song." She adds the small hospital pad with song lyrics and a pencil to the pile on the window sill.

"Thanks, Babe. This will help me make it through the night." Sonny takes a deep breath and coughs. Right on cue the 'graying professor' nurse appears for another breathing treatment.

"You better go on home and get some rest," Sonny tells his wife.

Jenny kisses him and strokes his cheek. "I love you. You know that, don't you?"

"I do," Sonny says, squeezing her hand before placing the oxygen mask over his face.

***

By Saturday afternoon Sonny is an expert at feeding himself and dispensing his own medication through his 'peg' tube. Jenny understands the process equally well and has actually 'fed' and 'medicated' her husband once at his request -- just to be sure she's confident.

Jake walks in during the Jevity 1.5 gravity flow part of Sonny's third feeding of the day. "Afternoon every--" He grabs his mother's arm at the elbow and pulls her from the room. "Mom, should I wait outside until he gets finished or what?" His face is red with embarrassment at this strange new situation.

Jenny pulls him right back into the room. His father sits relaxing in a chair, as if he were enjoying a meal; which, in a way, he is. "Howya doin', Son?" He offers his free hand as the thick, light-brown liquid trickles down inside the syringe he's holding. "Caught you off guard a little, huh?"

Jake approaches and shakes his dad's hand. "Wow, that's a sight! How does it feel, can you taste anything or..." He's still red faced, still getting used to this.

Sonny is fully dressed with the edge of his green Adidas T-shirt tucked up under his arm, showing his bare belly. He gestures with a stroke of his hand at the male nurse who is supervising this feeding session. "By the way, say hello to Thomas. Thomas, my son Jake."

Jake notices the man for the first time, having walked right by him a moment ago. "Oh, sorry. Howya doin', Thomas?" Jake offers his hand.

"Very well, tank you." Thomas answers in a Jamaican accent. His hand shake is firm but not finger crunching. He's a large bald black man with bulging arms tearing at the edges of his short sleeved purple scrub top. It's his turn to observe Sonny's feeding and make corrections if needed. "So far, so good, this aftanoon," he says.

In a few minutes Sonny is done and Thomas is away taking care of other patients. Jake says, "You have one more day, Mom tells me. I guess they want to make sure you've got the hang of it."

Sonny stands and yawns. His tube is taped to the side of his belly and his shirt is back down. "I've been walking the halls already." He coughs and spits into a Kleenex before walking over to lean against the windowsill. Sunshine is streaming in; the rain stopped during the night. "I'm afraid they'll be tired of me before tomorrow afternoon. Dr. O'Brien says three o'clock."

"Then you're done?"

"I still have to get a nebulizer from the drug store. I have to do my own breathing treatments, twice a day, for the next couple of months. And a visiting nurse will be coming around once in a while to make sure everything's going okay. So *done* may not be the right word. Let's say it's a good beginning."

Jack Teeter

Epilogue

Sonny and Jenny are back home. Back at the little white two-story farm house that sits on a long, narrow lot on North Street in downtown Brighton; a convenient and peaceful place to live.

Sonny is still writing songs. Some he writes in hope of fame and fortune, 'some he writes for fun, some he throws away and never plays for anyone', as the Statler Brothers song goes... But the most he writes for Jenny. And he sends the good ones to the United States Copyright Office -- just in case.

He's started a blog: 'Living on a PEG', to tell others about his experiences.

Sometimes the family comes over for Taco Night or the whole gang gets together for Beer and Pizza to watch the big game. Those times are hard: late at night, after Jenny's asleep, Sonny gets up and goes down to sit on that concrete bench in front of the library -- and watches the

trains go by.

THE END

https://livingonapeg.wordpress.com

Made in the USA
Columbia, SC
24 September 2022

67893650R00041